#JMTs
VOLUME 03

#JustMyThoughts

Can You Love Me ... NAKED?!

EXPERIENCED BY: NOVAH'S SON

#JustMyThoughts
Volume #3 | *Can You Love Me ... Naked?!*

Divinity

Honesty

Wholeness

&

Vulnerability

- - - - - - -

In any relationship!

The sacred soul of the feminine vibrates

a love for the Trinity of **SELF**.

It is through the depth of her experienced wisdom,

that she **CHOOSES** *to love you.*

                                             Without fear.

                                             Without lack.

                                             Through all doubt.

                                             Beyond childhood trauma.

                                             Transforming karmic cycles.

                                             Simply, because she chooses to.

                                             Never, because she needs you.

- - - - - - -

It is her Spirit & rare INNERGY
that creates an unconditional mastery.
A frequency that attracts as well as receives…
her true reflection in visible form.

DEDICATION:

To my inner child,

I honor your courage to see beyond the naked eye.

I value your truth, lived as wisdom in many lifetimes.

I admire the beauty you project inside out.

Thank you for choosing to BE LOVE!

xoxo

INTRO:

Til' You Do Right By ME...

Now even though you have some pretty damn good examples. You can't just give your ignorant and trifling ass exes all the credit for your BE - coming. Truth is… you allowed the lies, the cheating and stayed for years through the abuse. With an attempt to keep certain people around, you blindly thought were forever close to your heart. To others, you were just cherry-pickings and ripe ass!

To remain wholeheartedly dissatisfied and sexually suppressed in a comfort zone you had fucking control over! They possessed your ascendancy. "Power of the Pussy" my ass, young girl. Truth is… you dismissed the red flags for a superficial emotion and you ran from one relationship to another. With the same low vibrating insecurities. Never stopping to ask yourself, "what are you running from?" or "who are you searching for?"

TRUTH is... Til' you do right by YOU

Ain't shit nobody can say.

Ain't shit they gon do.

Ain't shit nobody else gotta prove.

You've been hiding love... From YOU!

It's YOU that needs to appreciate YOU!

Til' YOU, do right by YOU...

The flight to "healing" is delayed.

There's no need to chase what's already **WITHIN!**

- - - - - - -

Sincerely,

Your Soul

Nothing Outside of Me, Overpowers Me.

- - - - - - -

"What happens when you stop asking permission to be yourself?"

- Rachel Hollis

All Is Mind!

- - - - - - -

Ready to love, yet are you willing to INNER-stand …

What true love is?

I AM Safe Within Me My BE-ing!

- - - - - - -

To show vulnerability, highlight your strength!

Return to Sender & Transmute

- - - - - - -

Your heart will always tell you what you need.

Not what you want;

Pay attention to your heart!

Protect! Cleanse. Clear. Release.

- - - - - - -

Without mindfulness, intention is blinding.

Through mindfulness, actions are deafening.

Fill Your Own Cup, Then Serve!

In one split second.

I heard my heart fold.

Drop.

Shatter.

I was hurt.

Lost.

Trust Your Senses!

- - - - - - -

Full of vengeance and crude.

Through nonetheless, I still loved you.

Move With Purpose, When Guided.

- - - - - - -

I was confused.

Ignored.

Wandering.

The loneliest I'd ever been.

But nonetheless so were you.

-

In a time where we needed one another the most,

the pressure to remain secure was used

to conserve pride & harbor insecurities.

God is LOVE.

- - - - - - -

Today is a moment to reflect.

When everything changes because nothing's the same.

It's enough to prepare a loyal woman to go insane.

Fighting against instead of battling for.

Help me, help you rediscover the woman I used to adore.

Predictably worthless with you blaming me and me blaming you.

How can we go from saying "I'm done", to meaning "I do"?

-

I guess direction is what I'm trying to seek.

Whether it means making this work or leaving alone and bleak.

If I learn to talk and you learn to listen.

Maybe there'll be hope to keep "our forever" as the mission!

I AM GOD!

- - - - - - -

I AM, the Courage & Will of Release.

I AM, the Grace of Gratitude & Abundance.

I AM, the Depth of INNER-standing untold.

I AM, the Revelations of my ancestors that says, It's time…

I AM, the wisdom and blessings to UNFOLD!

-

I used to think in order to "silence the mind",

required for me to expunge or dismiss.

Over the last few months I've realized,

The silence is the key.

The silence ushers in peace of mind. The silence taps into intuition.

The silence discerns with understanding. The silence experiences patience.

The silence embodies gratitude. The silence isn't even silent at all…

It's refined by divination & soul cleansing.

Nothing Outside of Me, Overpowers Me.

- - - - - - -

"I don't believe everything happens for a specific reason.

I do believe it's possible to find purpose-even in the absence of explanation."

- Rachel Hollis

All Is Mind!

- - - - - - -

Make it make sense!

I AM Safe Within Me My BE-ing!

- - - - - - -

Go where the Spirit is purified with remembrance.

Where the mind is cleansed with transparency.

Where the heart's path is clear to lead the way.

Where the body knowingly moves, guided & protected.

Where the Soul is **FREE** to amplify manifestation.

Return to Sender & Transmute

- - - - - - -

WISDOM of the (past)

Never be afraid to learn or stop learning
with Your MIND & Your HEART!

Your mind does NOT know everything!
Once you think you've got the answers…

The questions then change.

Protect! Cleanse. Clear. Release.

- - - - - - -

EVOLVE through the (present)

Dive within DAILY and be patient with yourself.
Spending quiet time in 3 phases:

Meditation, Contemplation and Connection.

There's so much more to you that meets the naked eye.
Once you begin to see with your mind's eye,
remembrance, involution and faithfulness occurs.

Remembrance is key!
Through Remembrance ignites Involution.
Involution cultivates Faith.
The evolution of Faith, sustains Abundance!

(return to the WHOLE-listic purpose for living)

Fill Your Own Cup, Then Serve!

- - - - - - -

APPLY for the (future)

Everything you experience is ABSOLUTE!

As you let it flow, one remains prepared
with the wisdom to TRUST!

Be "willing", never sacrificed.

CONVEYING,
what has worked & what hasn't?

Courageous you are to fuel the spirit.
As others benefit immaculately!

Trust Your Senses!

In this FLOW,
I trust higher intelligence.

In this FLOW,
There is no room for fear, struggle or scarcity.

In this FLOW,
I Am the master not a servant.

In this FLOW,
I Am completely aligned with the Universe.

In this FLOW,
All is attracted through inspired action.

In this FLOW,
I Am Love.

In this FLOW,
I Am Energy.
I Am Growth.
I Am Joy.
I Am United.

Move With Purpose, When Guided.

\- - - - - - -

"I RELEASE WHAT NO LONGER SERVES ME!"

.
.
.

Say it with authority!
Say it with confidence!
Say it with power!

.
.
.

Say it as it is already done.

God is LOVE.

- - - - - - -

Spiritual Essence says "RISE UP like the Sun!"

I AM GOD!

- - - - - - -

Feel merciful,
Know wisdom,
Appreciate grace
and
Express compassion.

That's your androgen of Spiritual Love.

Nothing Outside of Me, Overpowers Me.

- - - - - - -

It is through self-love we choose honor.
Honor embraces a journey.

To journey with confidence,
We are **FREE** inside out.

All Is Mind!

- - - - - - -

For which I Am created,
I choose to Rise as well as Rest In Power…

ON EARTH!

I AM Safe Within Me My BE-ing!

- - - - - - -

To experience WEALTH,
I had to unlearn & relearn.

A relationship through God,
lead to inheriting my true Spirit…

Mind, Body & Soul.

Return to Sender & Transmute

- - - - - - -

Love is the ®evolution.

Protect! Cleanse. Clear. Release.

- - - - - - -

It's every time you go to the bathroom.

It's every time you pass gas or cough.

It's every time you sneeze.

It's every time you blow your nose

Every time you inhale deep, or yawn to exhale.

Every time the body does something naturally ... We release.

Fill Your Own Cup, Then Serve!

- - - - - - -

Embody
The
Kinda
Love
That
Does
Not
Ask
Her
To
BE
Anyone
Other
Than
Who
She
Is.

Trust Your Senses!

Here's the thing …

We are
ALL CALLED,

yet respond in
Divine Time.

Move With Purpose, When Guided.

- - - - - - -

I asked for grace.
I received ease.

.

.

.

For that,
I AM Grateful!

God is LOVE.

- - - - - - -

You can make waves with just a little ripple.

I AM GOD!

- - - - - - -

Lean into what IS,

as we do not "need" anything…

We are required to BE.

Nothing Outside of Me, Overpowers Me.

- - - - - - -

Uplifting oneself.

    Pull out unexpressed emotions.

        Releasing childhood resentment.

            Pull out abandonment trauma.

                Releasing truth.

                    Pull out a birthright to BE.

                        Allow oneself to go deep.

All Is Mind!

- - - - - - -

When you know, you know.
If you don't, you'll see.
All you want is attentive.

AS YOU ARE.

I AM Safe Within Me My BE-ing!

- - - - - - -

Choose to **BE** - Loving through Words.

Choose to **BE** - Grounded by Action.

Choose to **BE** - Magnetic with Soul.

Return to Sender & Transmute

Words are Influential.

.
.

Hands are Rejuvenating.

.
.

Soul is Luminous.

Protect! Cleanse. Clear. Release.

- - - - - - -

.
.
.
.
.
.
.
.
.
.
.
.
.
.

Because you made the decision,
Transformation has already unfolded.

Fill Your Own Cup, Then Serve!

Gratitude discovers a radical enchantment,
each day with every experience.

Trust Your Senses!

- - - - - - -

I Am brave enough to affirm,
I AM HOME!

Move With Purpose, When Guided.

- - - - - - -

Feed.
Nurture.
Expand.

Lead as the heart. - **Foundation**
Speak from the heart. - **Nourish**
Serve with the heart. - **Evolve**

God is LOVE.

- - - - - - -

A connection to Source, innovates truth.

I AM GOD!

- - - - - - -

You will not have to choose between that which you **CREATE**!

Nothing Outside of Me, Overpowers Me.

- - - - - - -

For so long I allowed others to dictate my life.

Cultivating alignment
with the HIGHEST form of Self
was essential before wandering.

All Is Mind!

- - - - - - -

Syncing
The
Mind
With
The
Heart
Inspires
Magic
AND
Miracles.

I AM Safe Within Me My BE-ing!

- - - - - - -

Self-Love is a fundamental pillar to Universal Harmonization.

Return to Sender & Transmute

- - - - - - -

An expression of love, mastery and joy assures, I AM!

Protect! Cleanse. Clear. Release.

- - - - - - -

When experiencing unfamiliar energy,
Connect within and ask your heart for cleansing.

BE open to receive clarity.

Follow your intuition.
A familiar path will form guiding you to **LIGHT**.

Fill Your Own Cup, Then Serve!

- - - - - - -

Where Meditation flows, Power vibrates.

Trust Your Senses!

- - - - - - -

Power is in the LIGHT of the hands!

Move With Purpose, When Guided.

- - - - - - -

Limitations and restrictions
only shows just how
disconnected one may be.

God is LOVE.

- - - - - - -

LOVE is not restricted nor controlled.

I AM GOD!

- - - - - - -

YOU hold keys that will unlock an authentic reality.

Nothing Outside of Me, Overpowers Me.

- - - - - - -

I will not dim my light!
I Am willing to pass you some shades.

All Is Mind!

- - - - - - -

Life is NOT about the rollercoaster,
so why would we focus on the destination?

Rather than allowing ONESELF
to create gratitude amongst the ride.

I AM Safe Within Me My BE-ing!

- - - - - - -

In the midst of fire,
I walked alongside my Shadows
and decided not to gaze in their gray skies.

Realizing,
I AM THE LIGHT!

Return to Sender & Transmute

- - - - - - -

Because our brothers & sisters
Don't look like us in this lifetime,
We refuse them Christ consciousness.

We diminish our faith.
Lapse judgment.
Project fear.
Promote conflict within.
Raging war.

What sad hell to live as …

Exuding battles around us that may only
BE "ONE" WITH LOVE.

Protect! Cleanse. Clear. Release.

- - - - - - -

Activating my light,
graces me clarity
to see beauty
through the depth
of my wisdom.

LIGHT A PATH

Fill Your Own Cup, Then Serve!

- - - - - - -

Ironically,
We are all headed in the same direction.

PURPOSE.

Trust Your Senses!

- - - - - - -

Curse unto others
Misguided projections. Distrusted actions.
Miscommunication. Assumed knowledge.

Gift unto others
Asks the tough questions.
Get comfortable with being uncomfortable.

Curse unto self
Unspoken subconscious.
Hindered truth. Perceived blockages.

Gift unto self
Break barriers.
Repels toxicity, Protects the aura.

The key is to trust intuition & practice discernment.

**OBLIVION:
A Gift or A Curse**

Move With Purpose, When Guided.

- - - - - - -

Masculinity is not complicated to sustain.
Yet we must first remember our femininity.
Captivating & Grounded.

THE TWIN FLAME

God is LOVE.

As she stood there brushing her teeth,
peering back at herself in the mirror.

She was reminded of what it felt like to seek freedom.
Yet, feeling burdened by her own existence.

Desire gave her patience.
Mindfulness guided her with grace.

Her heart then whispered out to the flesh of her womb.

Calling forth a golden light.
Encircling the death of survival.

Grasping ancestral lines.
Connected. Originated. Karmic.

Melting into a spiral of release, forgiveness & healing.

Grounding anew.
As the energy of crystals rebirthed love within!

Karmic Release

I AM GOD!

For a long time,
I envisioned myself as that little girl,
standing at the end of the driveway.
In front of her childhood home.

The only home my parents owned.
The first place I ever had my own bedroom.
A space where I allowed my imagination to fly.

I questioned, "Where is home?"
I wondered "What does home look like?"

.
.
.

Suddenly I realized.
It's an emotional feeling,
not a physical place.

I Feel Home.

Nothing Outside of Me, Overpowers Me.

- - - - - - -

PEACE.

Where unity meets, to divine and experience truth.

All Is Mind!

- - - - - - -

Am I searching for what may never be seen?

I AM Safe Within Me My BE-ing!

- - - - - - -

Though I've been hurt a thousand times before,

nothing fills agony
more than losing
what enlightens
and
nurtures the soul.

Return to Sender & Transmute

- - - - - - -

I never want to be torn between
accepting what once was
and
fighting to be whole again.

Protect! Cleanse. Clear. Release.

- - - - - - -

Lend me your ear, as I seek passion.
Lend me your eyes, so that I see clarity.
Lend me your arms, to cloak in balance.

Fill Your Own Cup, Then Serve!

- - - - - - -

I tend to think faster than the world around me.
Building anticipation. Reflecting anxiety.

Trust Your Senses!

We choose to fall in love,
Then wonder why war conflicts within.

Move With Purpose, When Guided.

- - - - - - -

It's safe to know,
sometimes it couldn't hurt
to just walk away
when all else fails.

God is LOVE.

- - - - - - -

Truth be told,
death is instantaneous
the minute you acknowledge
you've fallen.

I AM GOD!

- - - - - - -

The heart knows fury,
when overwhelmed
with significant emotion.

Whom shall I fear?

Nothing Outside of Me, Overpowers Me.

- - - - - - -

As told best by nature, life requires
a little nonsense for entertainment.

I'm not entertained.

All Is Mind!

- - - - - - -

Crossroads do not determine
the pleasures of an expedition.

A path chosen without fear,
meets gratification.

I AM Safe Within Me My BE-ing!

- - - - - - -

There's a reason for everything.

Surrounded by that reason,
there's ten more views
one feels the need to express.

Return to Sender & Transmute

Freedom
is neither love nor war
until it's experienced as:

Uncertain,
Alluring,
Compelling
and
Complicated.

Honor what just is with conviction.

Protect! Cleanse. Clear. Release.

- - - - - - -

Love
Plunges
Through

The
Heart,

When
Syndicated
With
Unity.

Fill Your Own Cup, Then Serve!

- - - - - - -

Love expressed
without fear,
without temperance,
and
with honorable devotion;

Is defeat or triumph?

Trust Your Senses!

- - - - - - -

To learn from all experiences in life,
without judgment.

Dissolves disillusions.

Move With Purpose, When Guided.

- - - - - - -

How could bliss not be apparent?

God is LOVE.

- - - - - - -

Whether in partnership or controversy;
of any kind, there's love.

I AM GOD!

- - - - - - -

INTENTION:
Authenticated with trust.
Breathing as truth.

Nothing Outside of Me, Overpowers Me.

- - - - - - -

If it's jolly, the heart beats effortlessly.

All Is Mind!

- - - - - - -

*With no indiscretion, I closed my eyes
and opened the gift of another.*

I AM Safe Within Me My BE-ing!

- - - - - - -

Raised
By
The *Wolves*.

Nurtured
By
The *Eagle*.

Return to Sender & Transmute

- - - - - - -

To set me on fire, burns through your lies.

ALCHEMY OF THE SOUL

Protect! Cleanse. Clear. Release.

- - - - - - -

*I have the courage to release
those things that I no longer need
and that are preventing me from growing*

Fill Your Own Cup, Then Serve!

- - - - - - -

TRUST:
The basis of all relationships.

Trust Your Senses!

- - - - - - -

Once it's sparked within,
you awaken aspiration
from its slumber.

Move With Purpose, When Guided.

- - - - - - -

Stop processing the process.

God is LOVE.

- - - - - - -

It may appear different going up,
then it will feel coming down.

I AM GOD!

- - - - - - -

Set your world free of judgment!

NOTES

NOTES

NOTES

NOTES

www.ingramcontent.com/pod-product-compliance
Lightning Source LLC
Chambersburg PA
CBHW071406080526
44587CB00017B/3194